Anatra e la colorazione oca libro

Coloring Pages for Kids

**All rights reserved. No part of this document may be reproduced
Used or transmitted in any form or by any means, electronic or otherwise. This means you
cannot photocopy any material ideas or tips that are provided in this book.**

Coloring Pages for Kids
An imprint of Ciparum LLC

Anatra e la colorazione oca libro
© 2017 Ciparum LLC
All rights reserved.
ISBN-10:1-63589-478-6
ISBN-13:978-1-63589-478-3

Coloring Pages for Kids

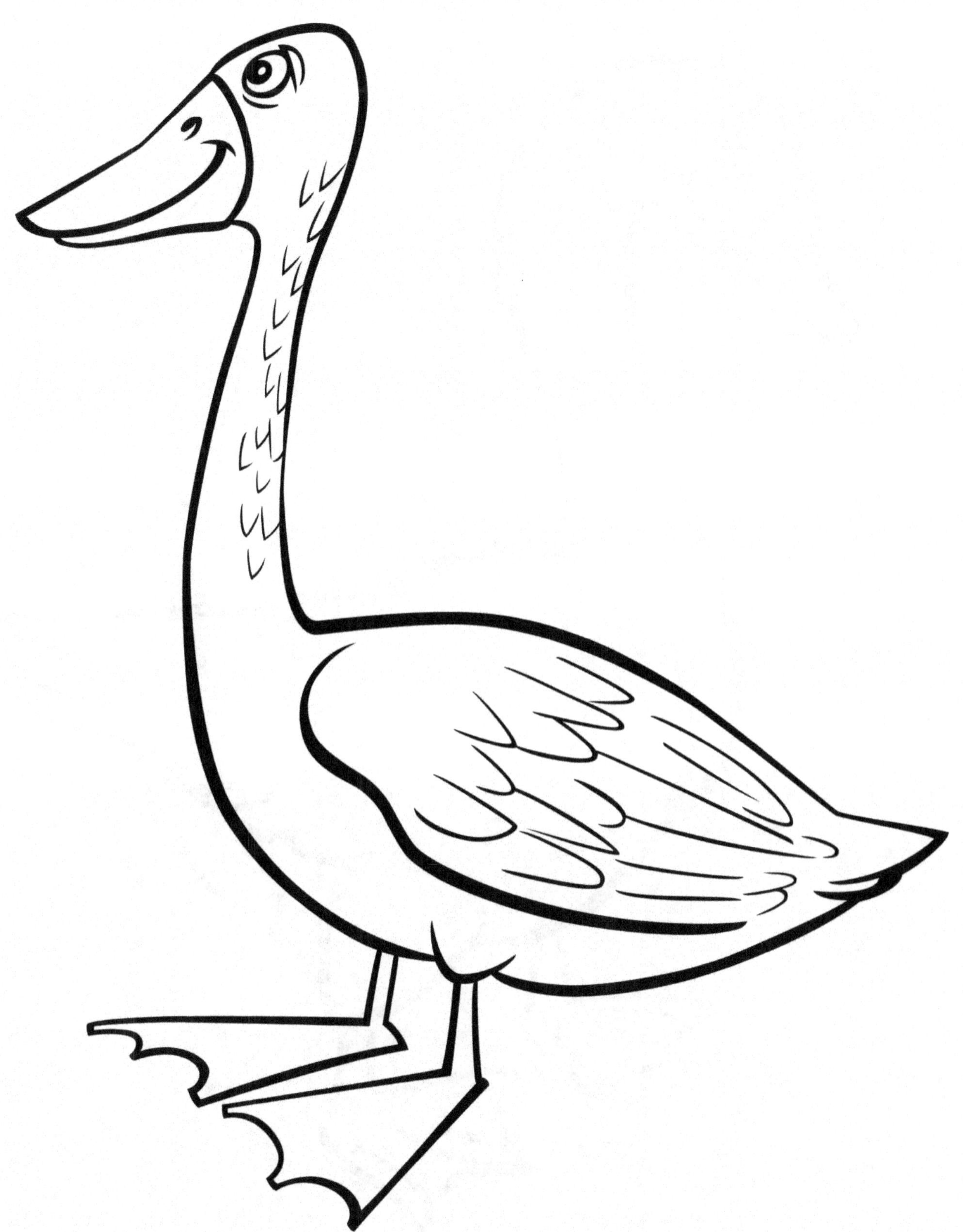

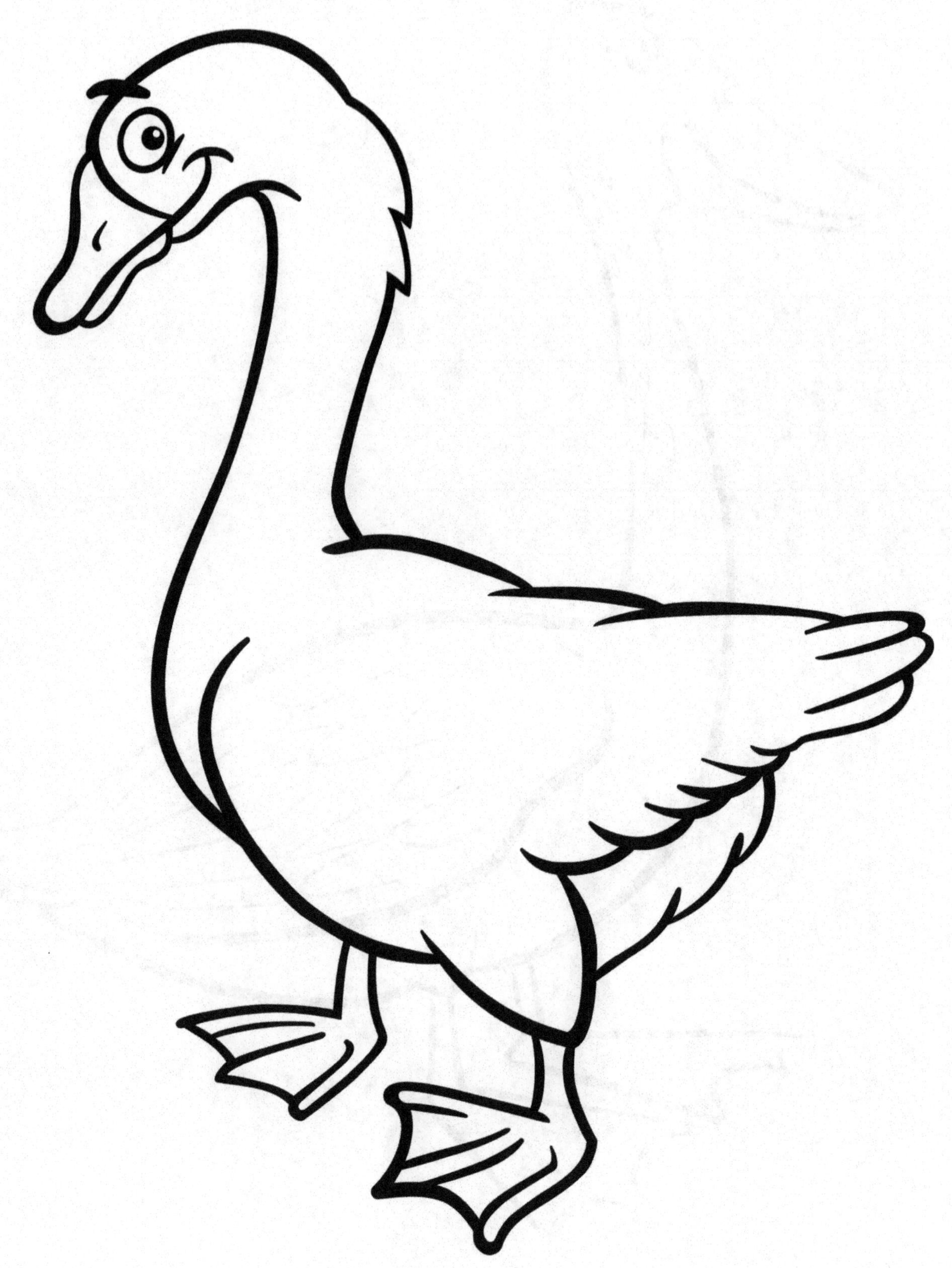

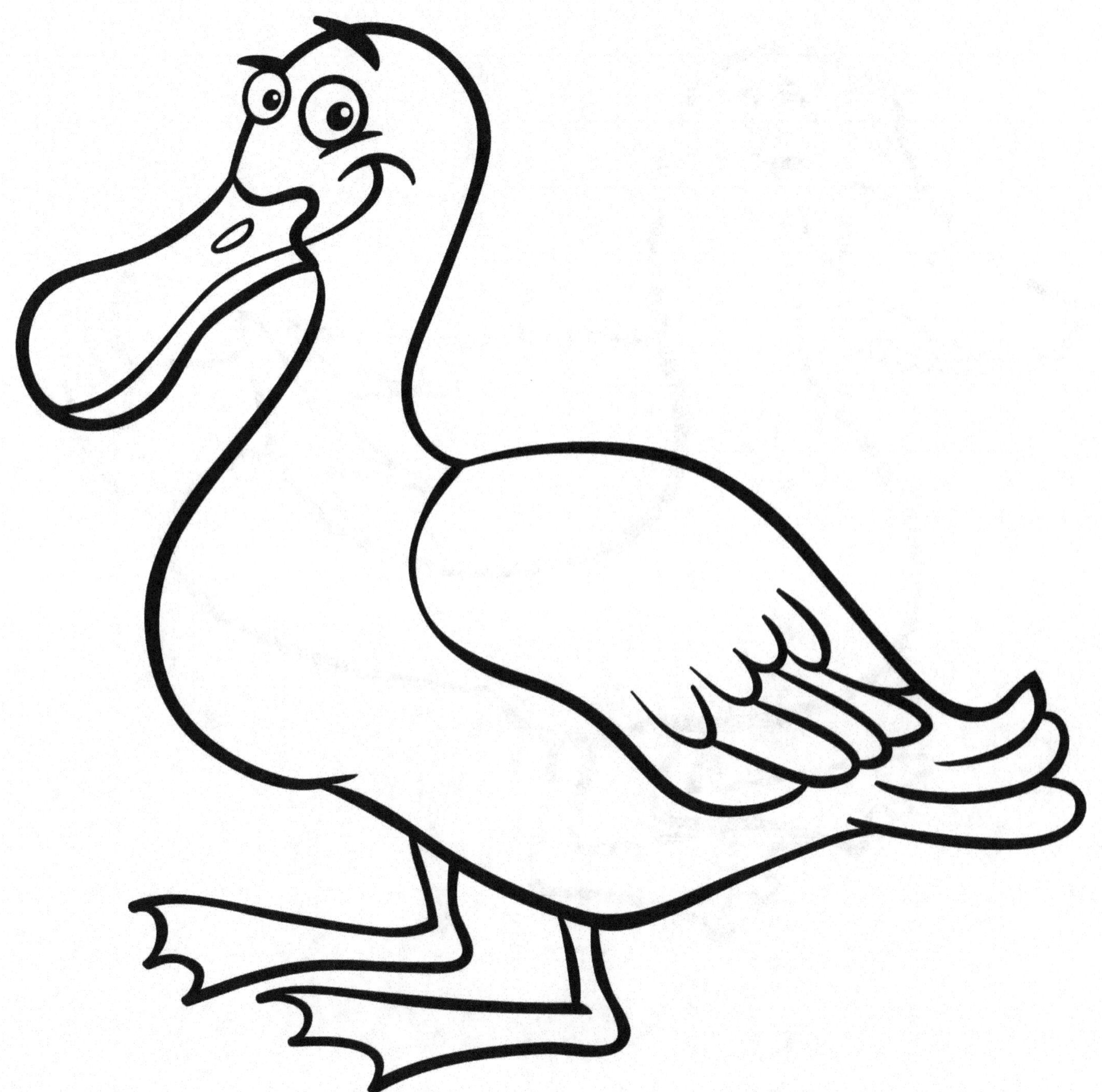

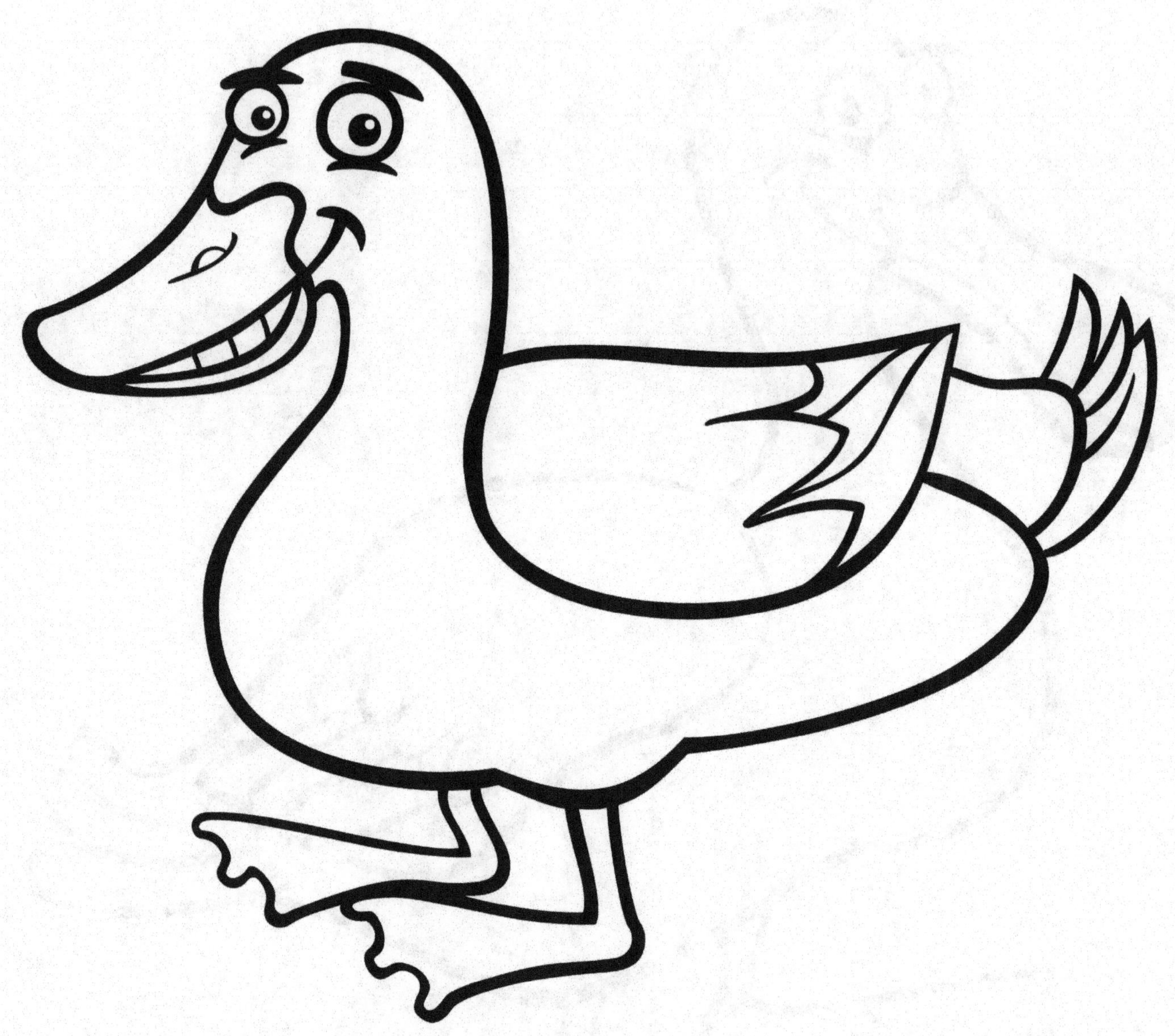

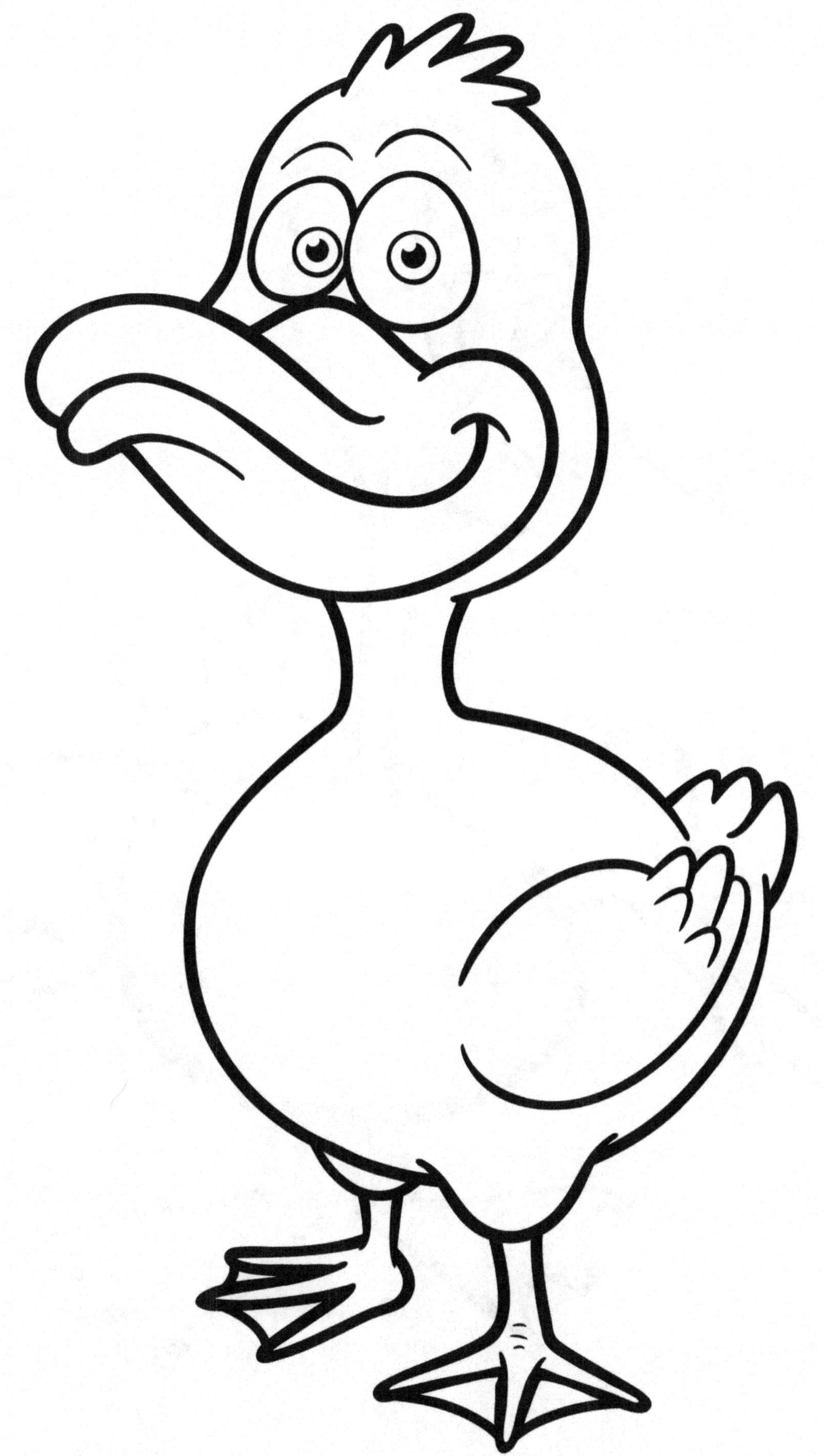

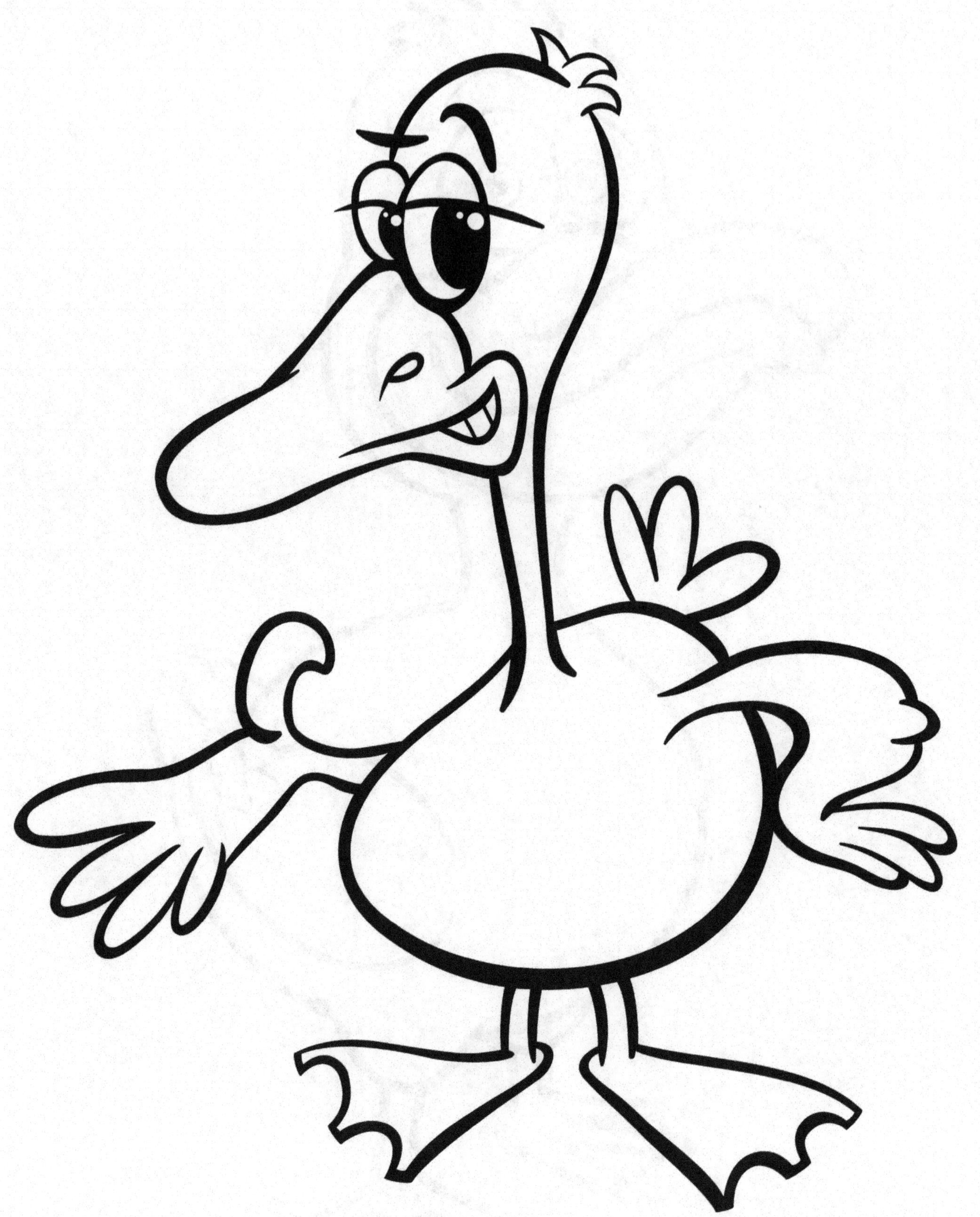

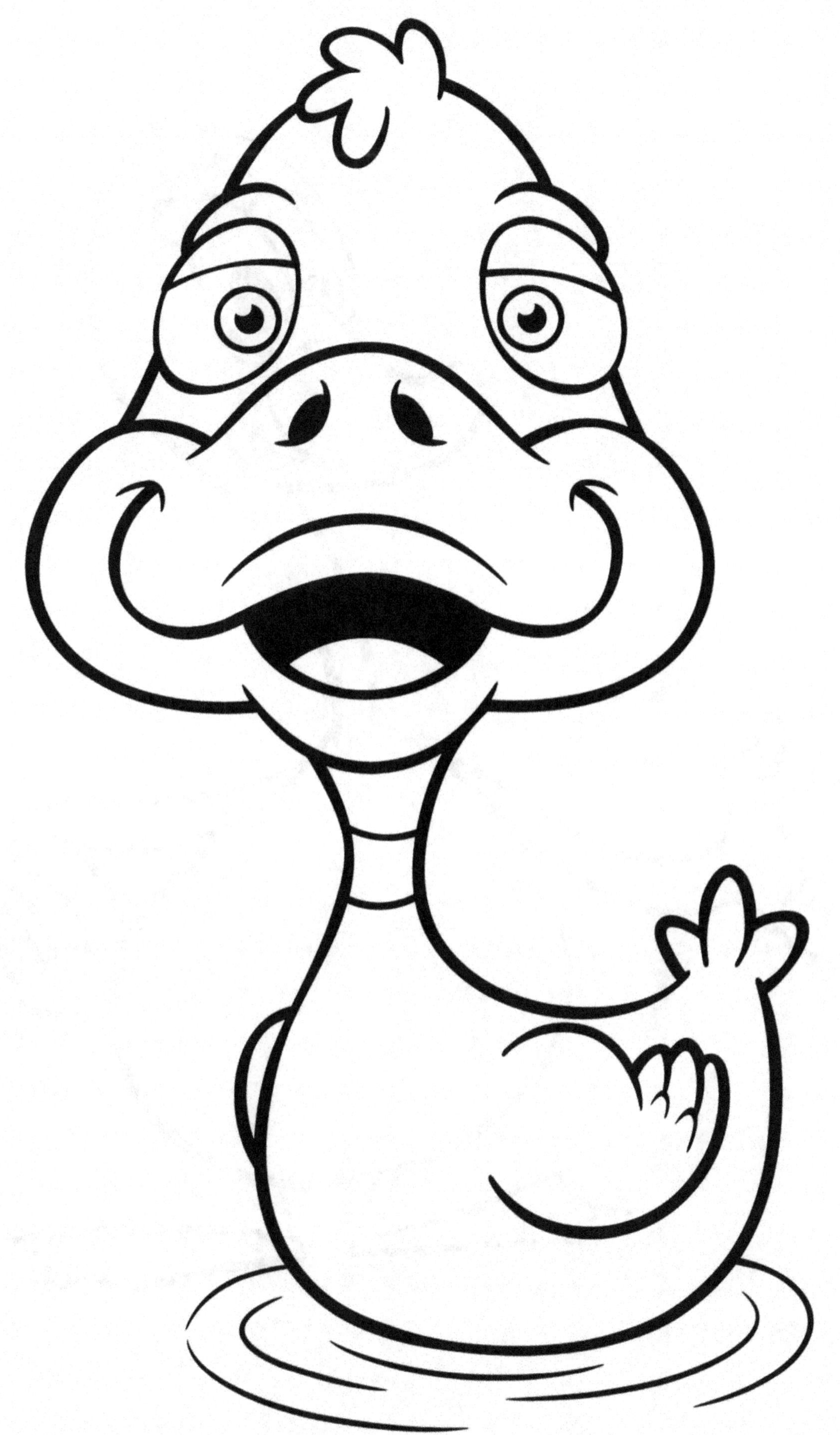

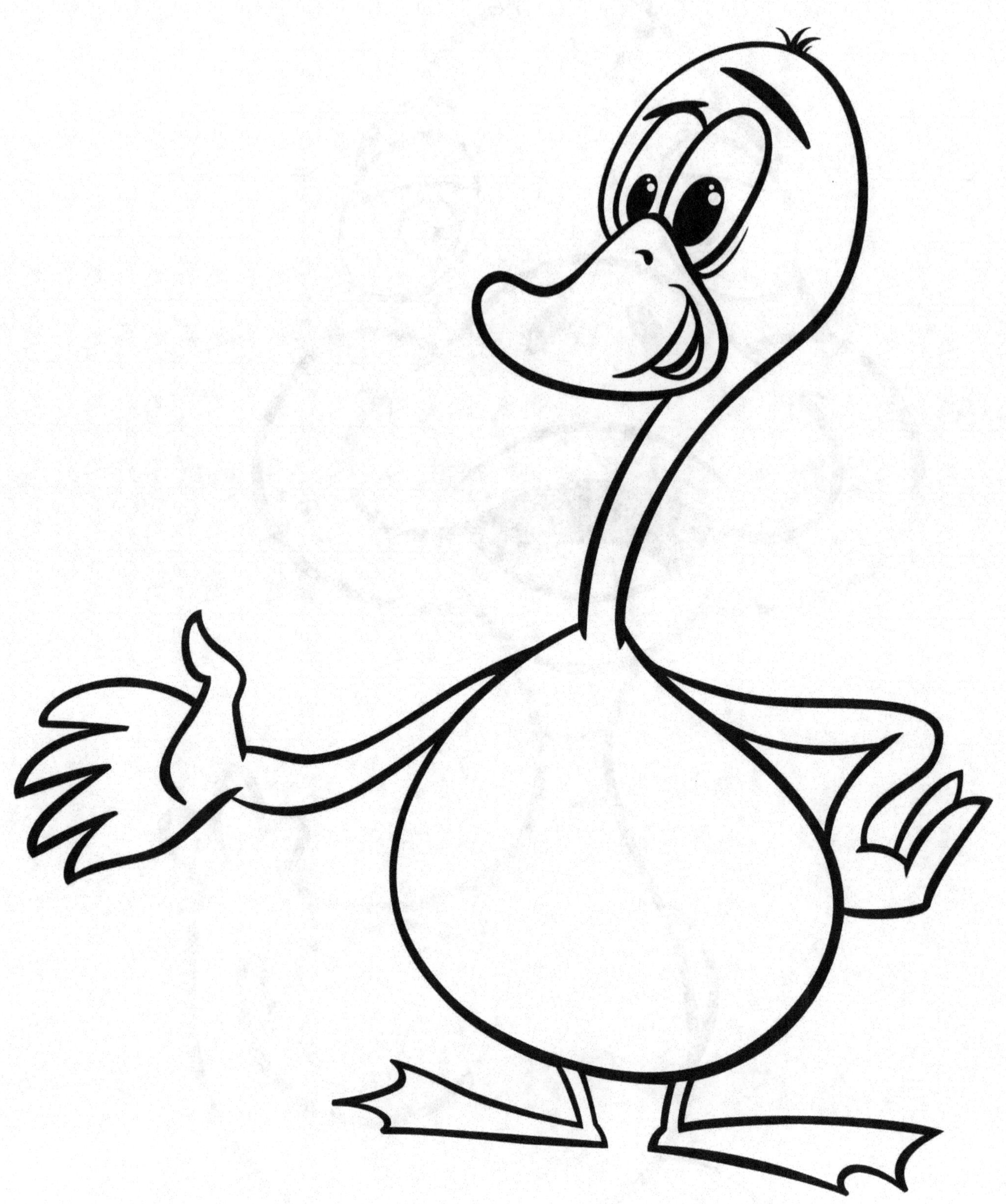

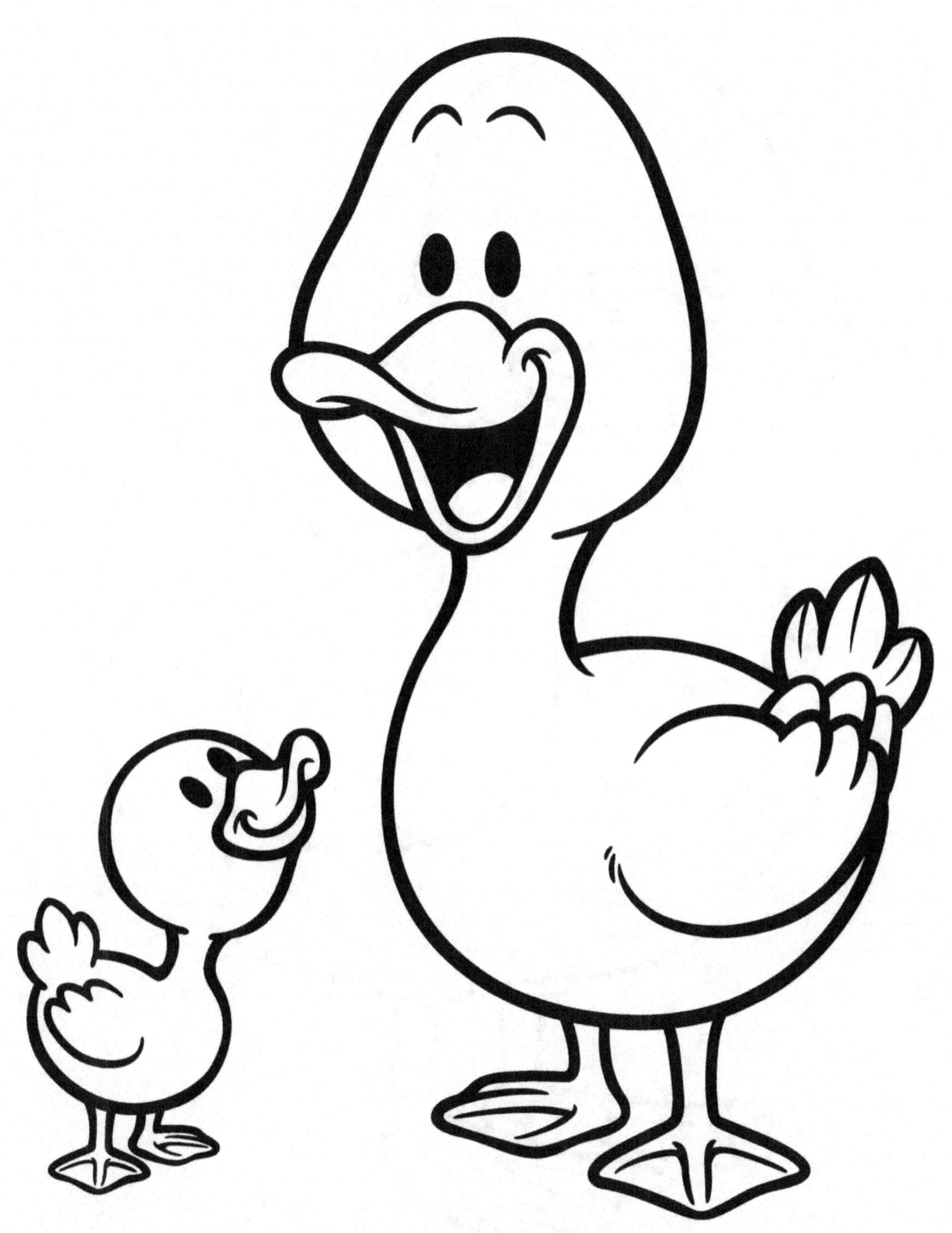

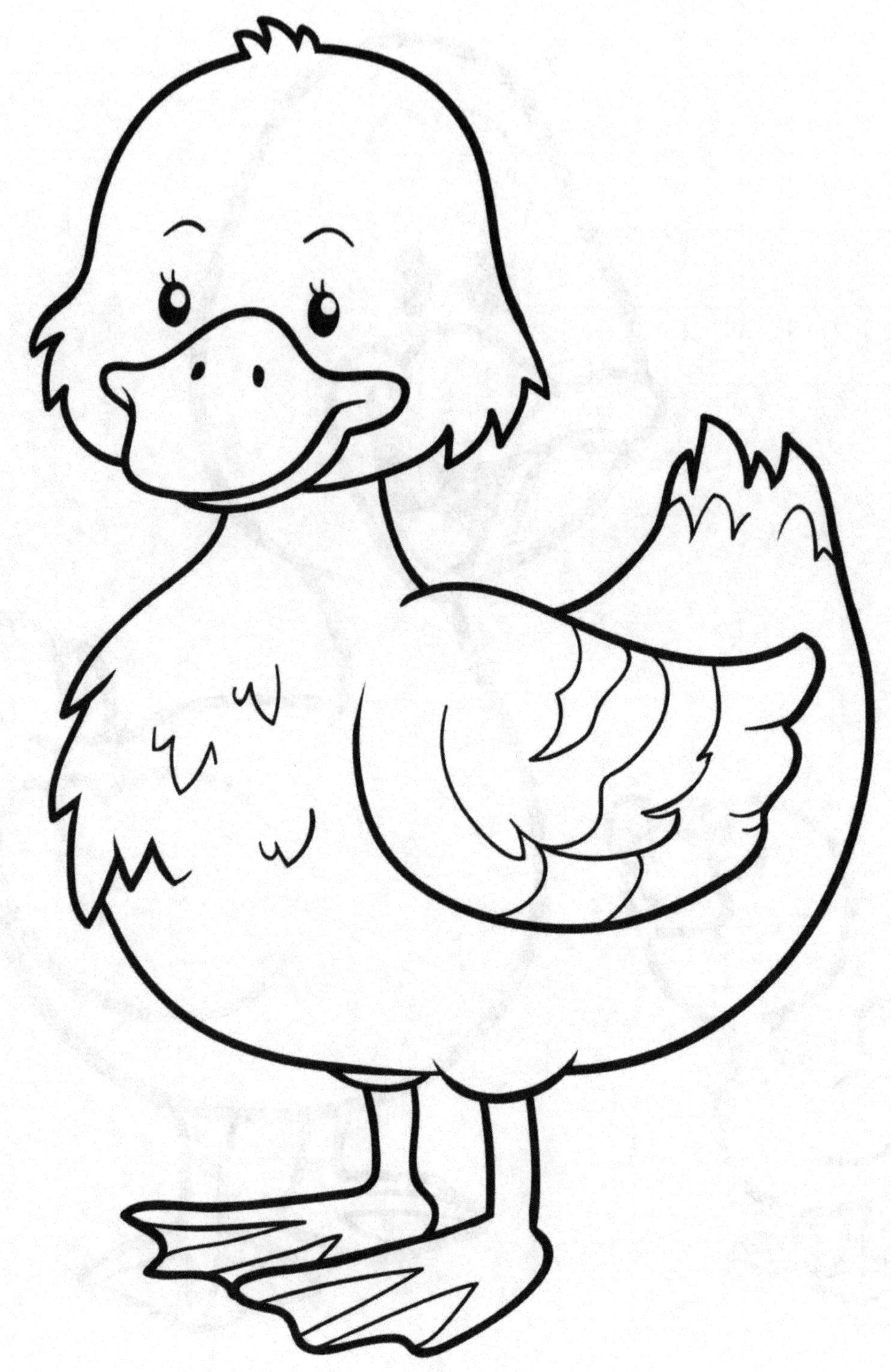

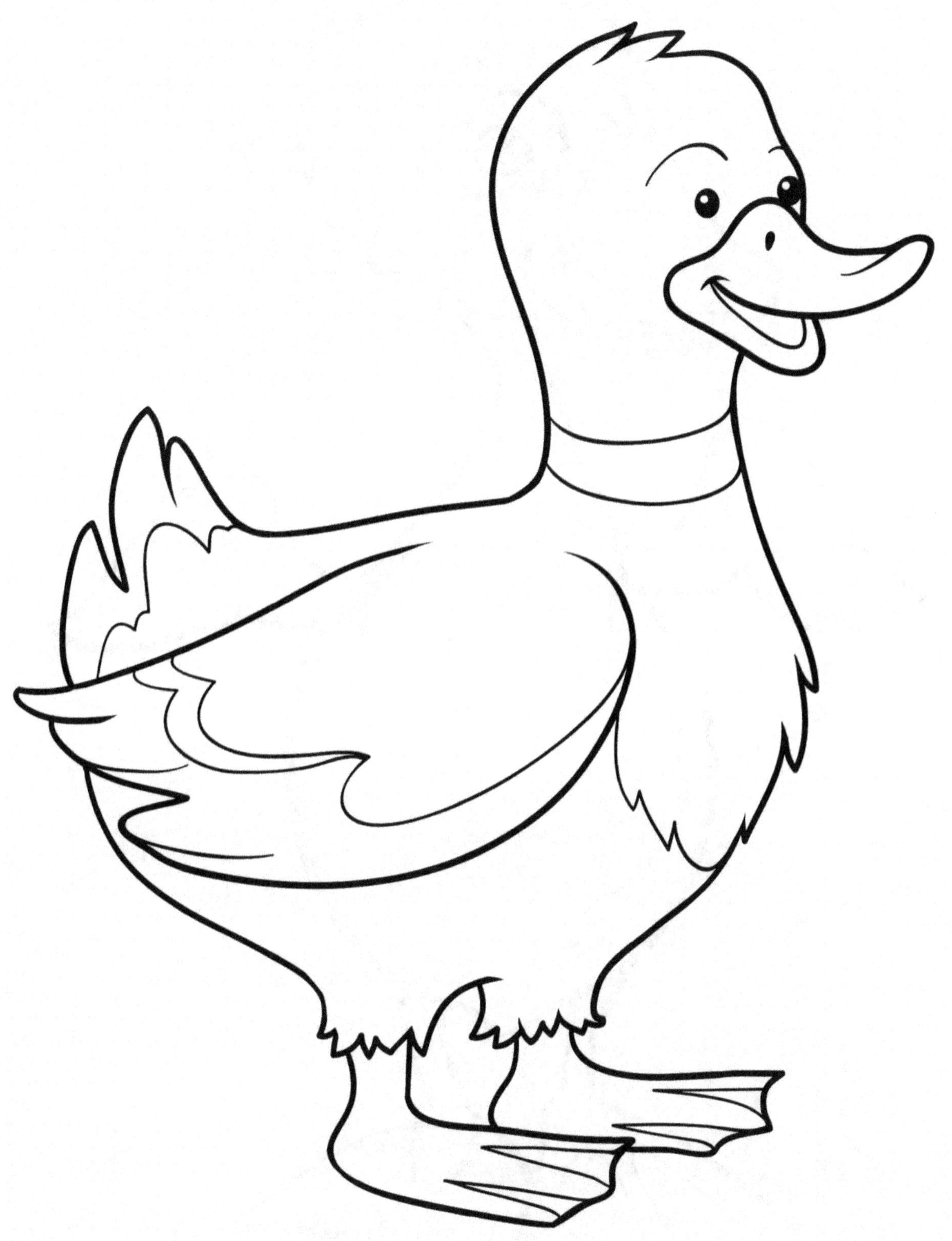

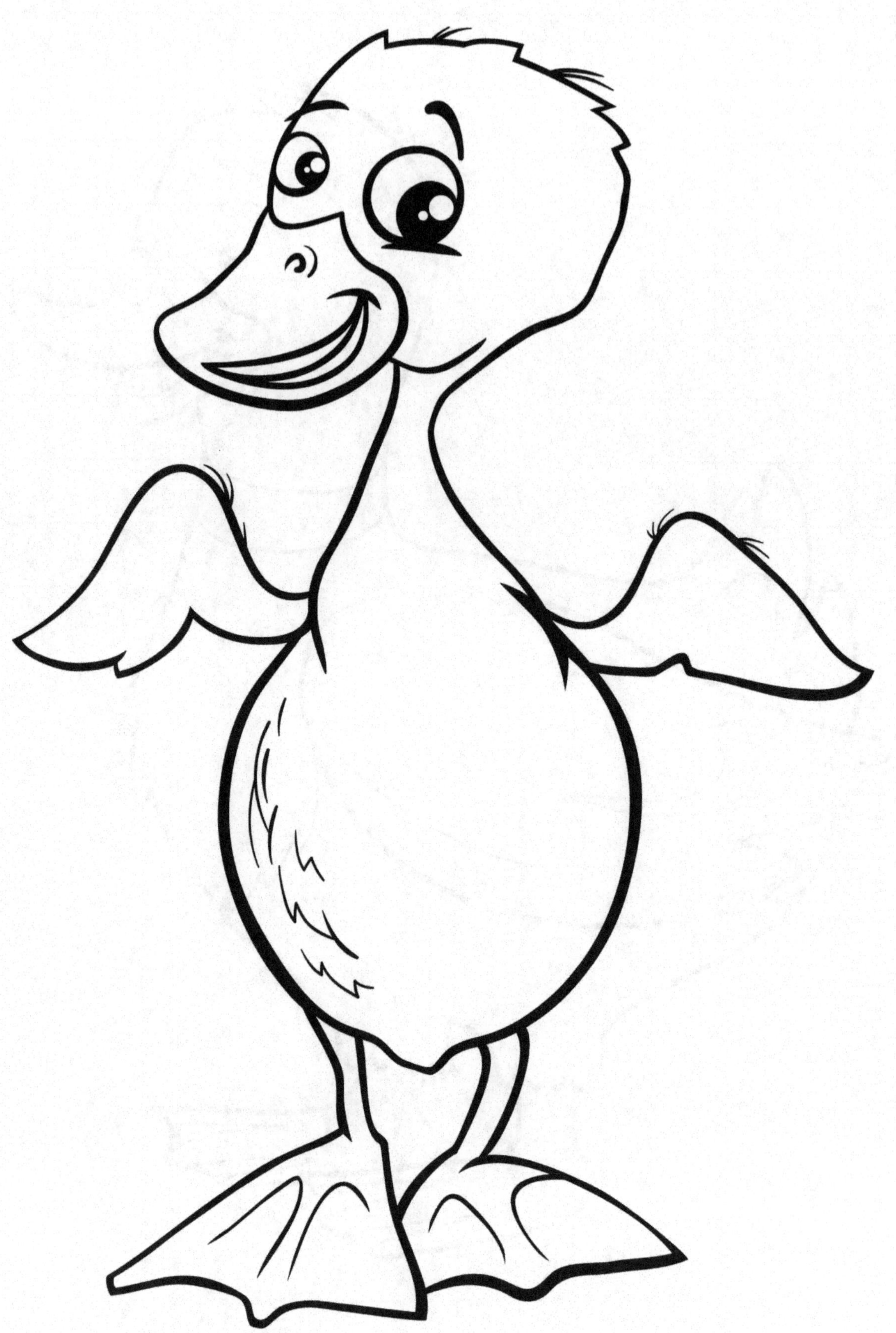

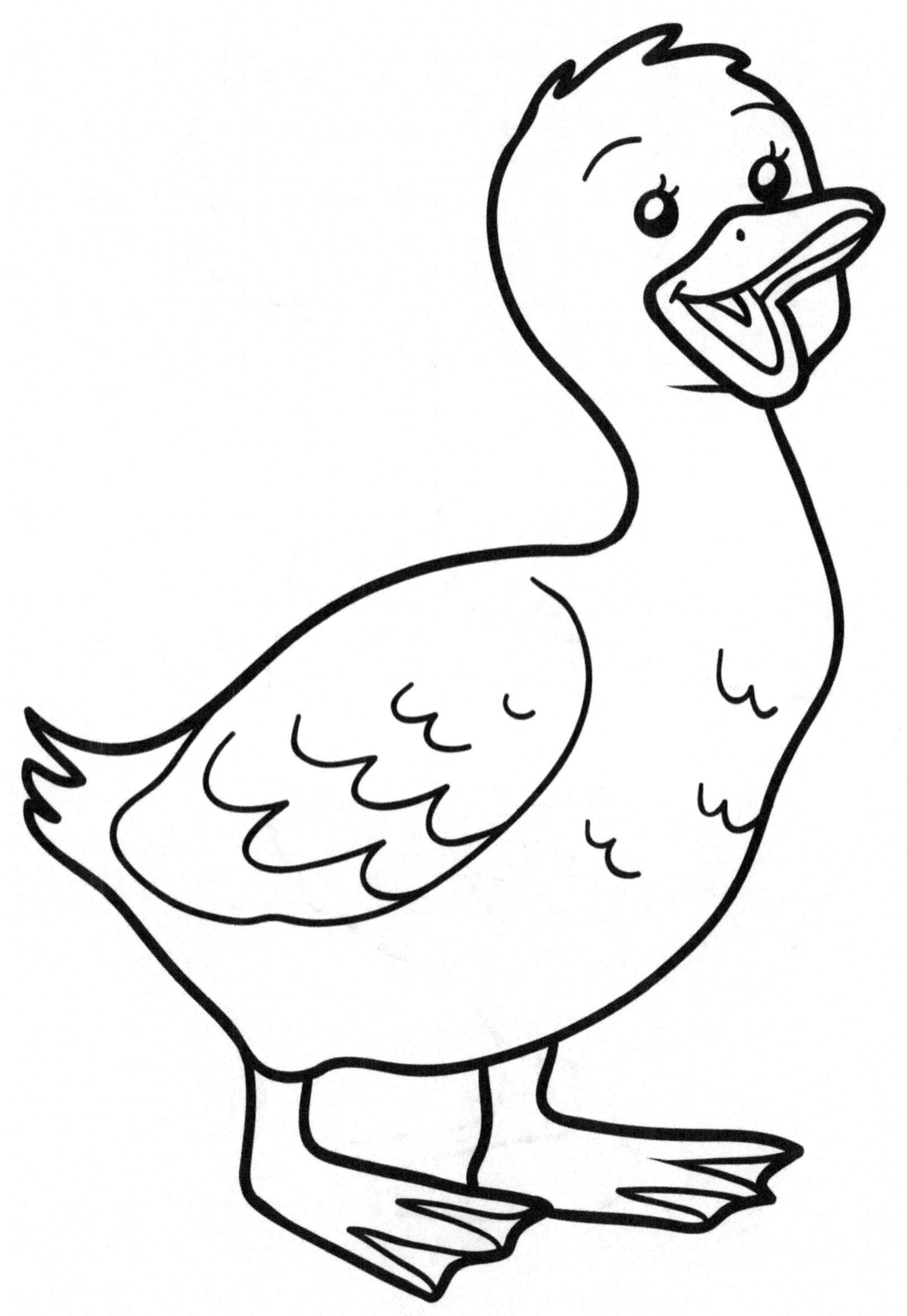

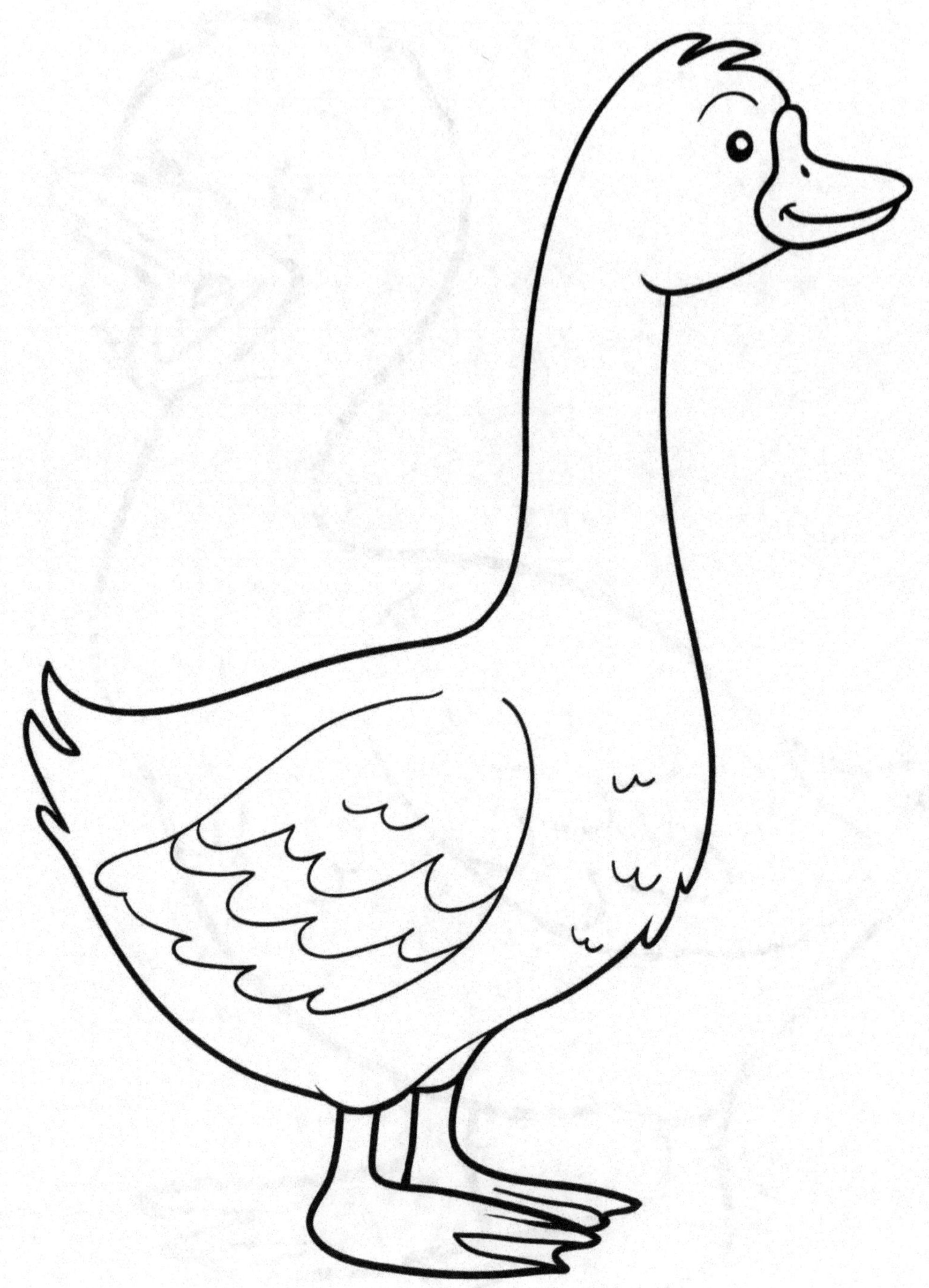

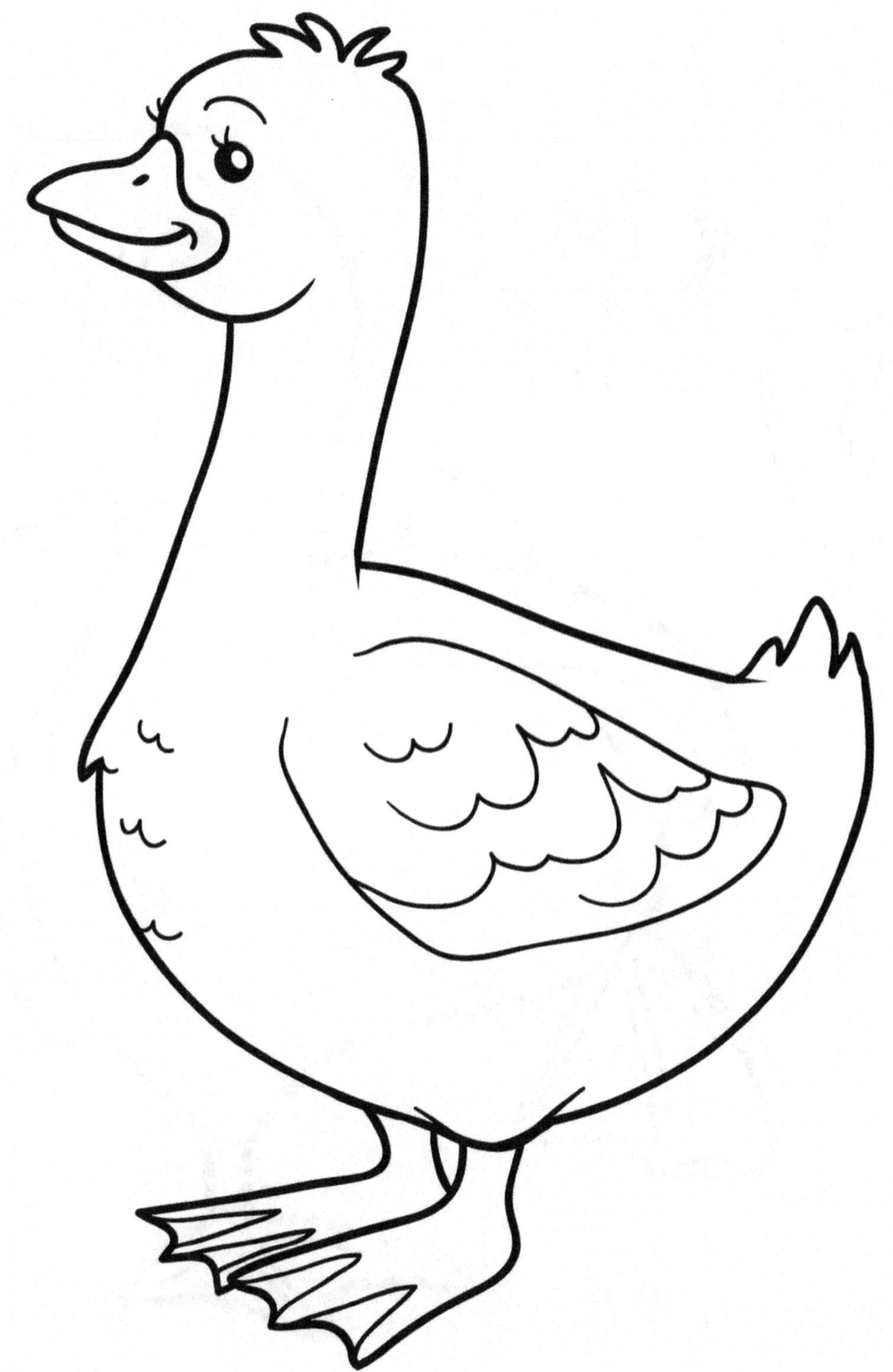

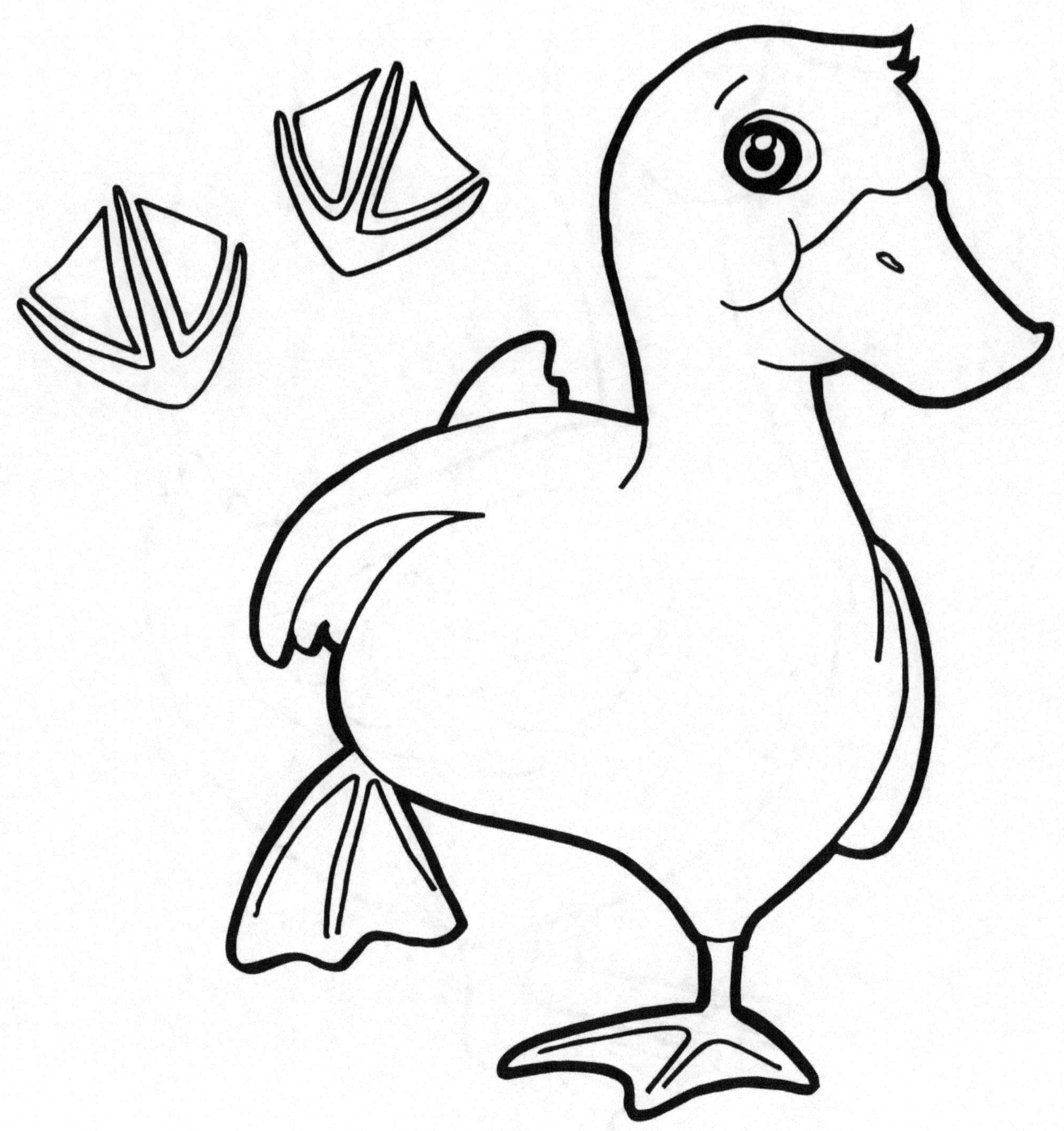

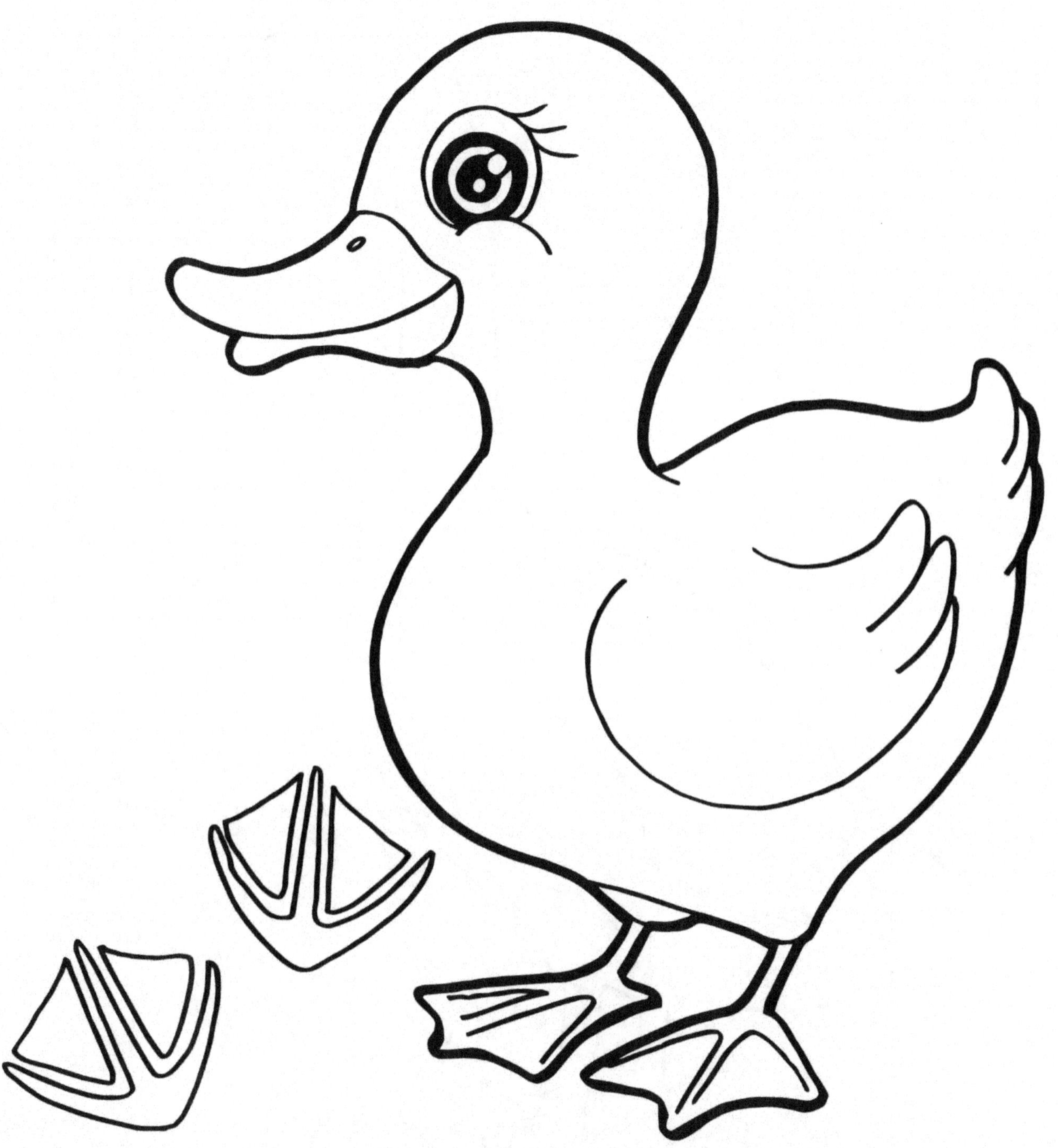

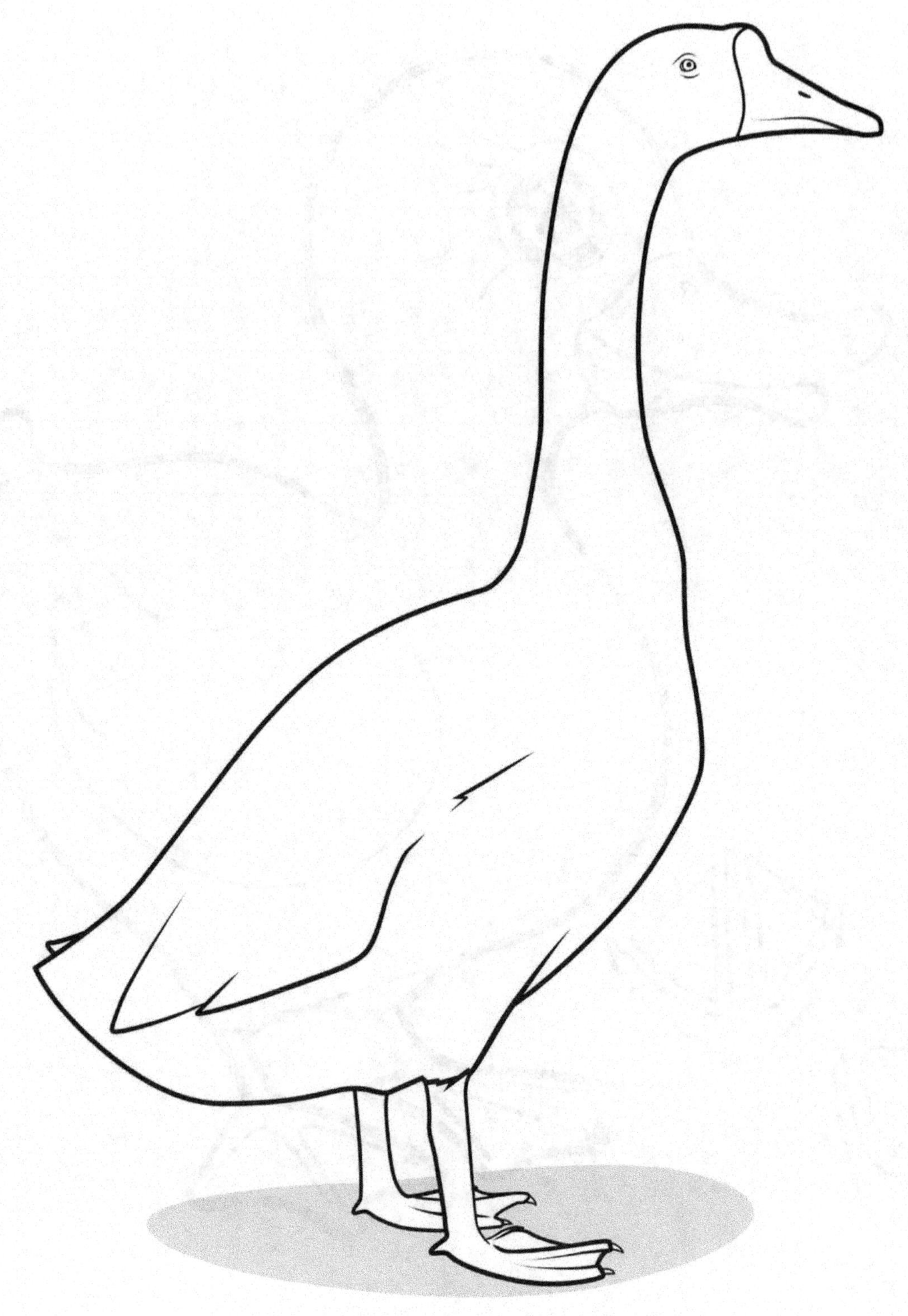

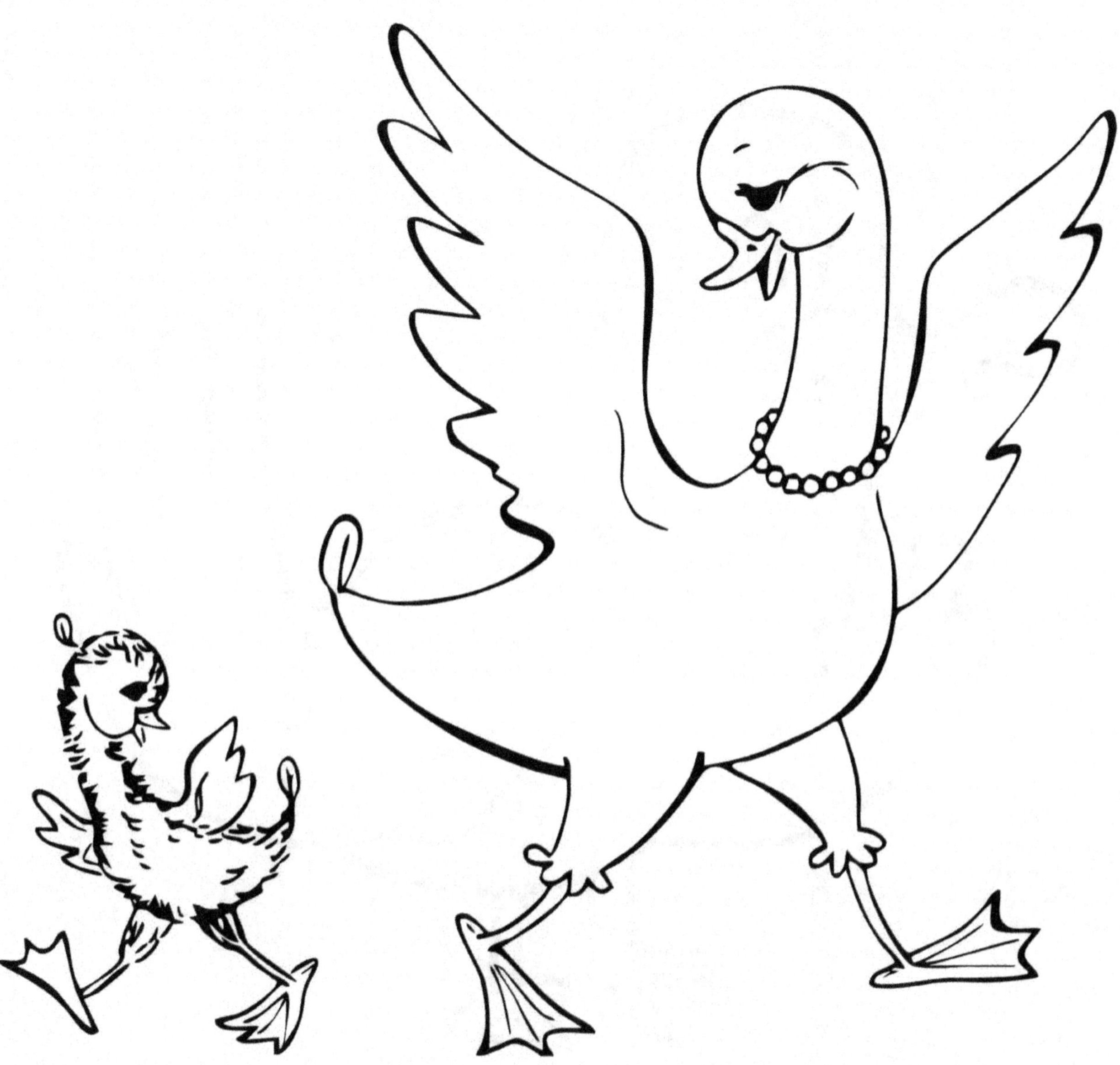

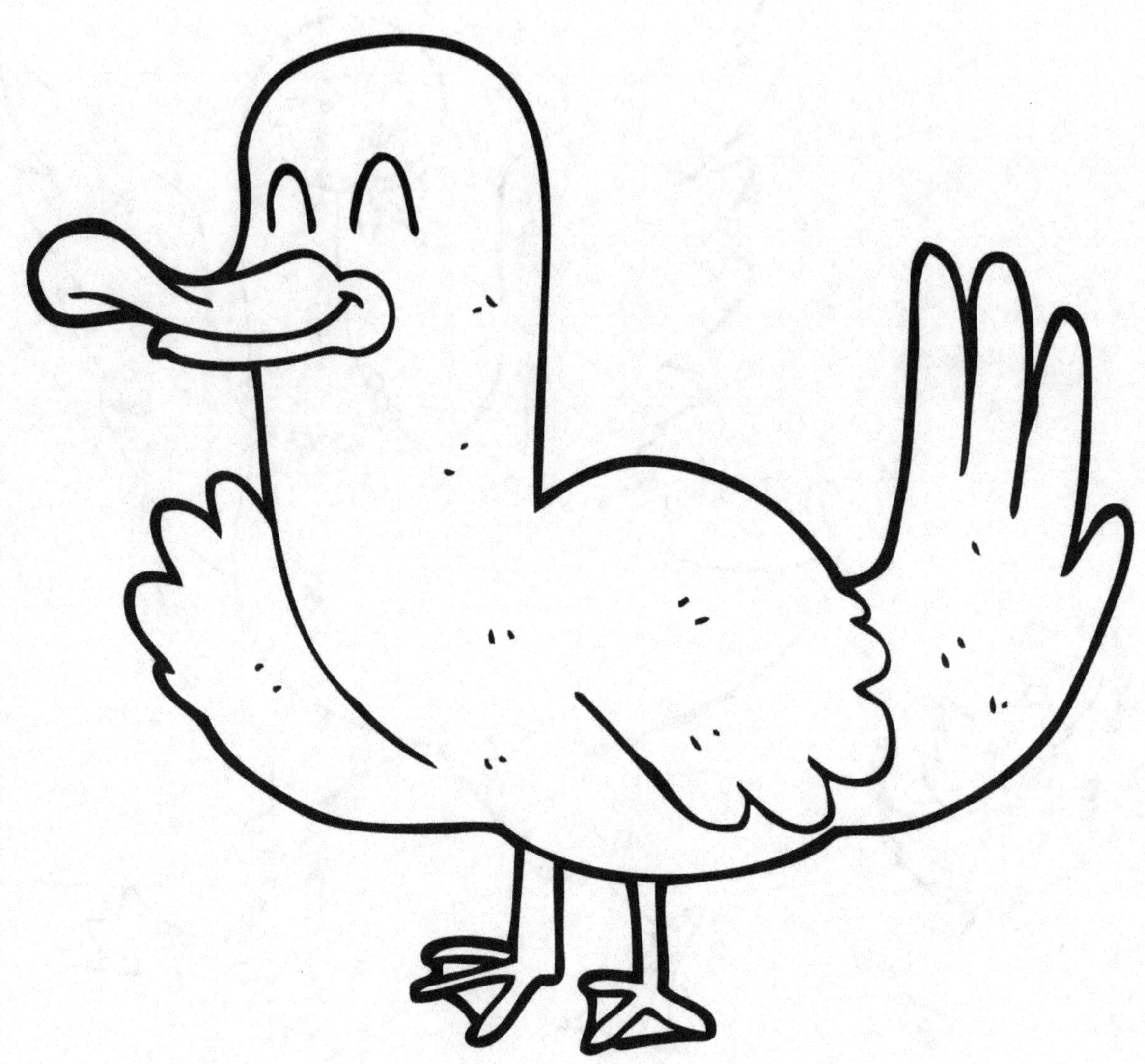

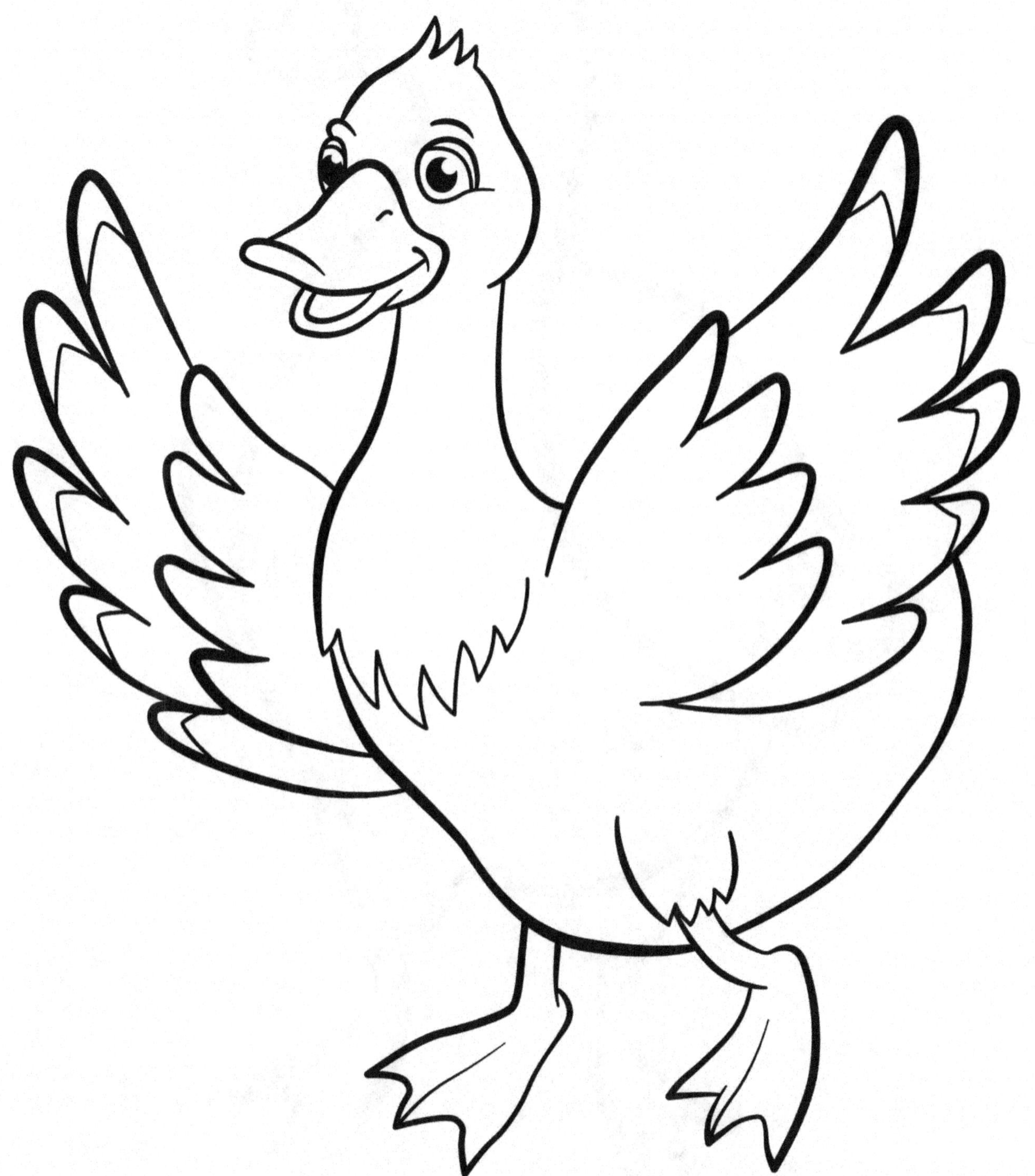

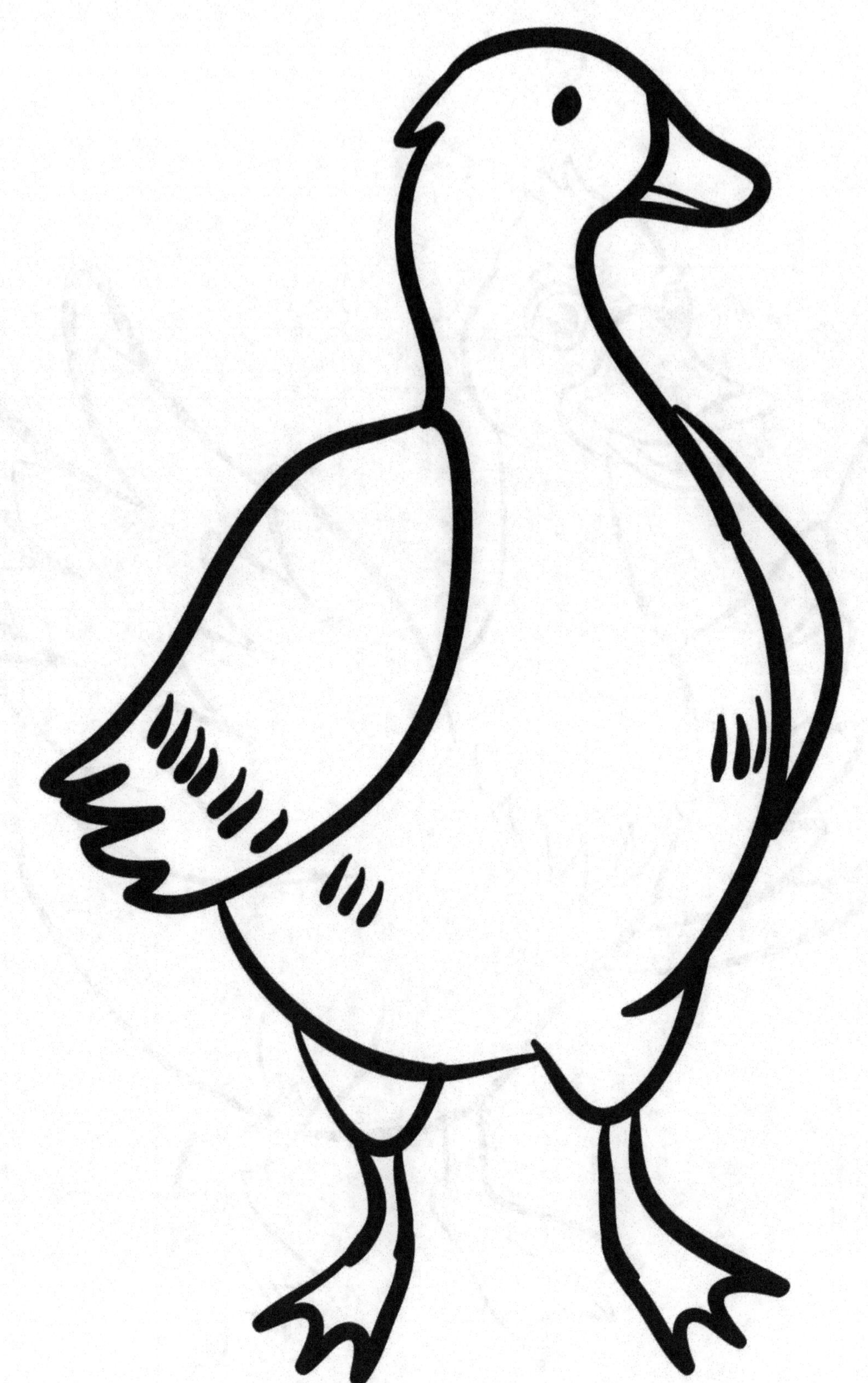

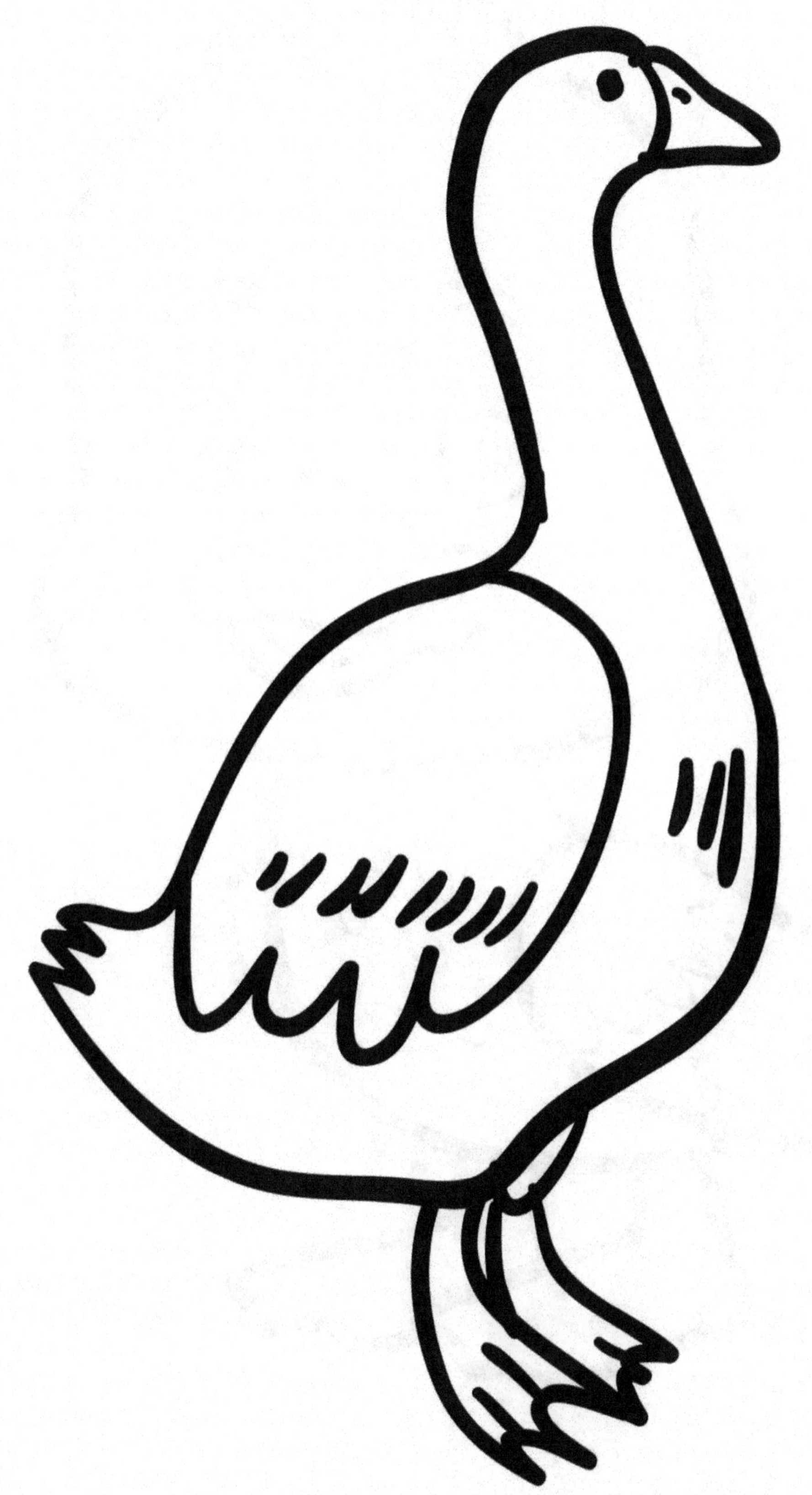

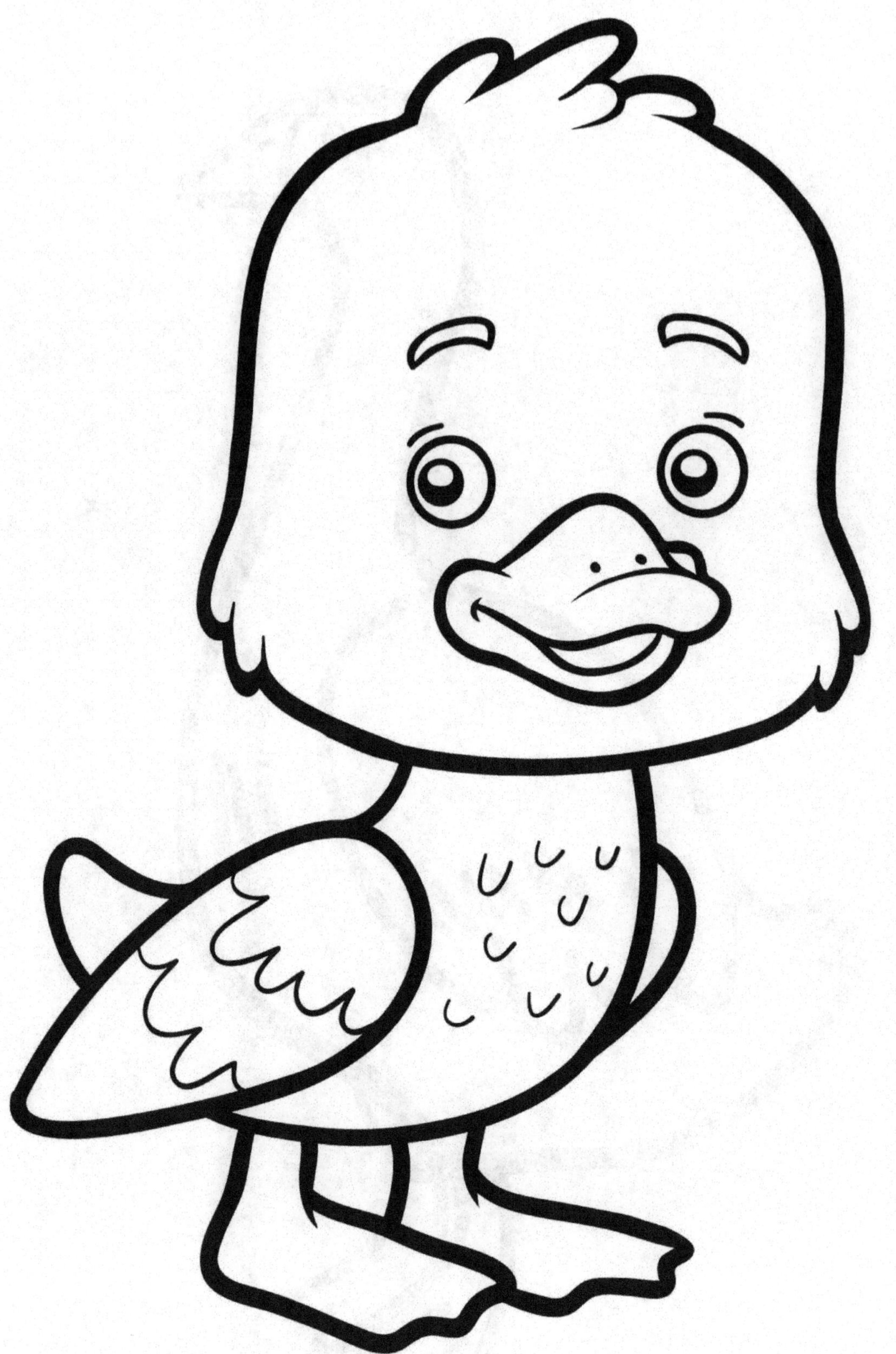

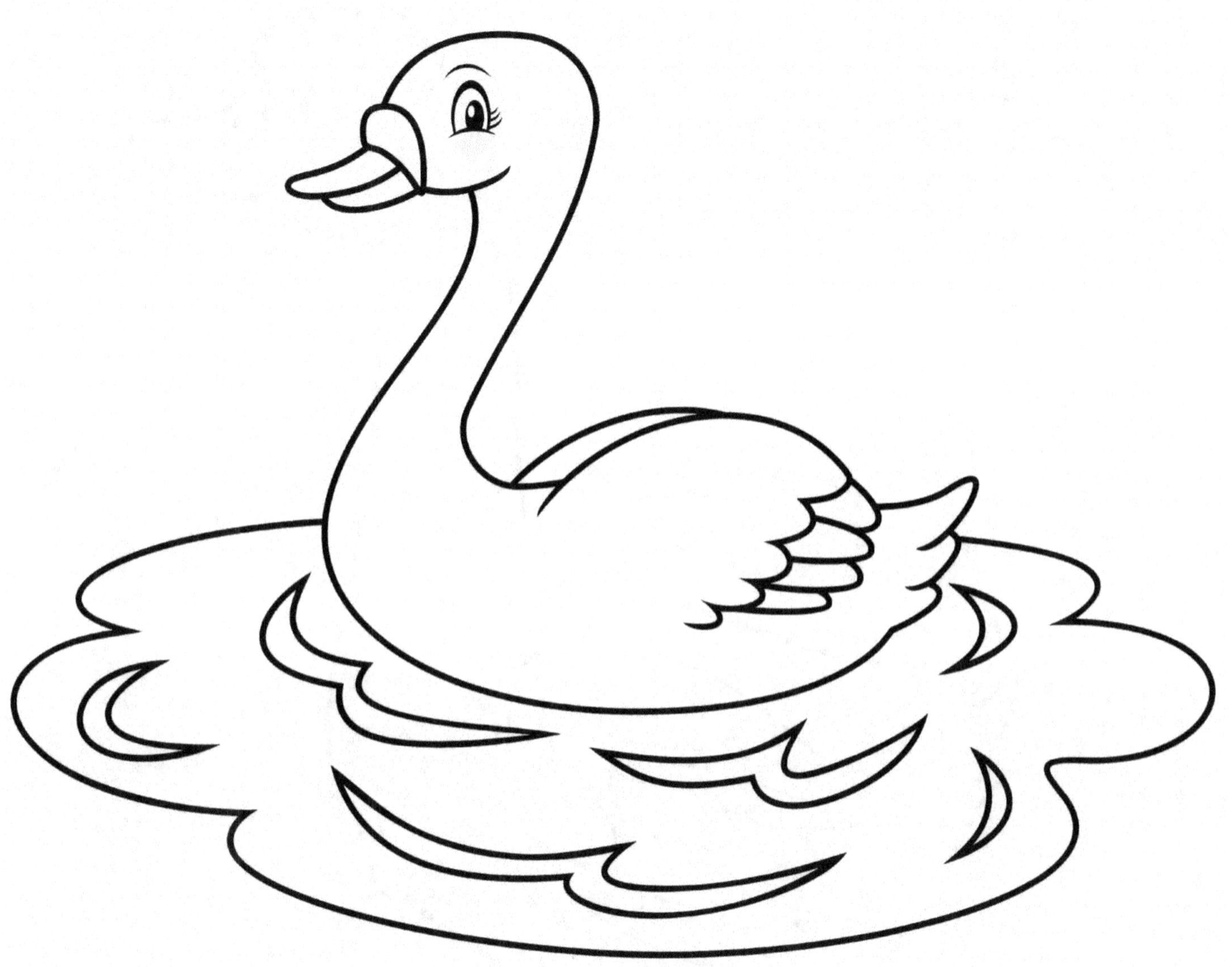

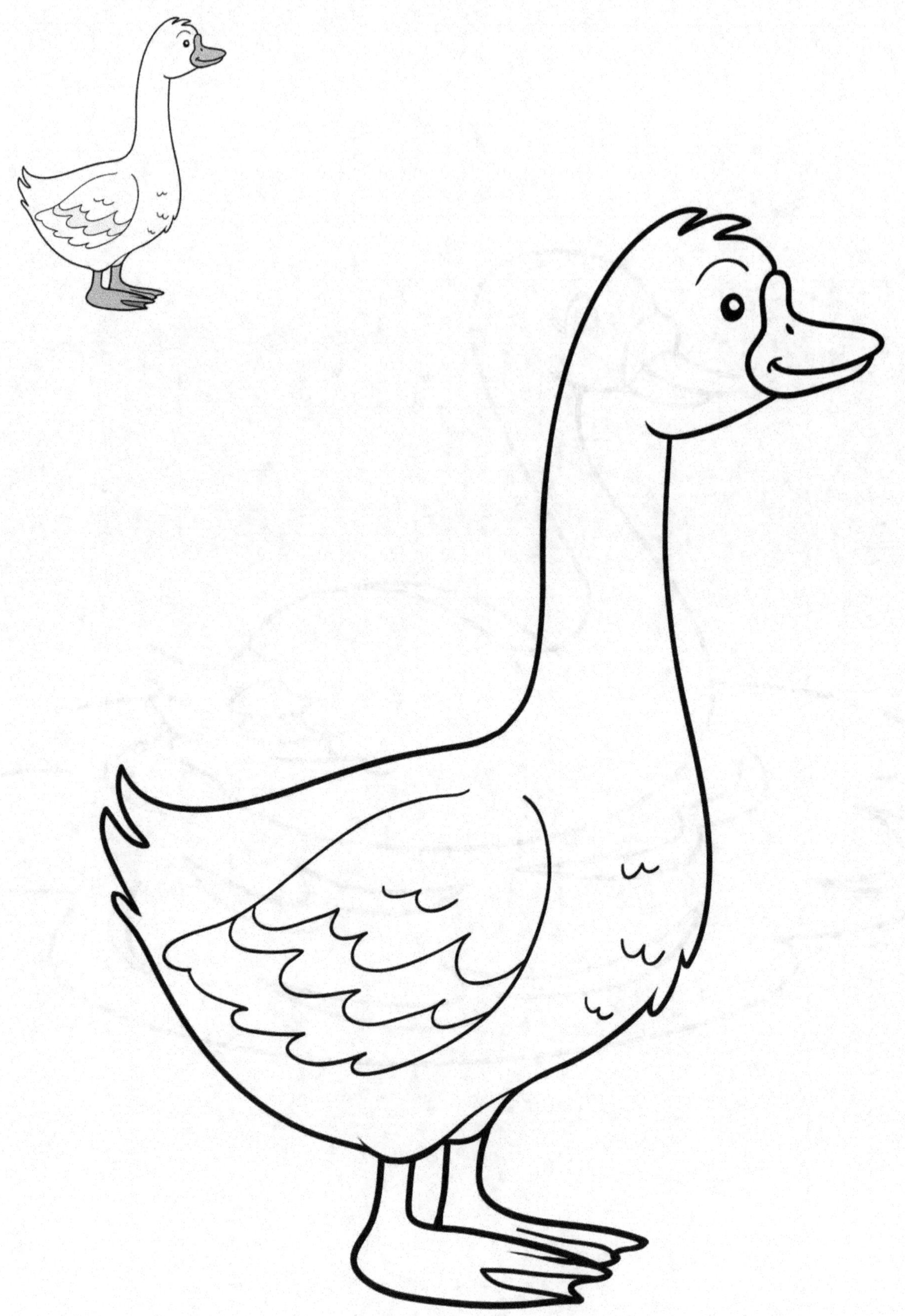

www.ingramcontent.com/pod-product-compliance
Lightning Source LLC
Chambersburg PA
CBHW080321030726
47593CB00009B/2836